Robert Downey Jr.

ABDO
Publishing Company

Big Buddy BOOKS
Buddy Bios

by **Sarah Tieck**

VISIT US AT
www.abdopublishing.com

Published by ABDO Publishing Company, PO Box 398166, Minneapolis, Minnesota 55439.

Printed in the United States of America, North Mankato, Minnesota.
102013
012014

 PRINTED ON RECYCLED PAPER

Coordinating Series Editor: Rochelle Baltzer
Contributing Editors: Megan M. Gunderson, Bridget O'Brien, Marcia Zappa
Graphic Design: Maria Hosley
Cover Photograph: *AP Photo*: Evan Agostini.
Interior Photographs/Illustrations: *AP Photo*: Evan Agostini (p. 8), AP Photo (p. 15), Starpix, Marion Curtis (p. 21), NBC, Heidi Gutman (p. 13), Peter Kramer (p. 23), PatrickMcMullan.com via AP Images (p. 13), Chris Pizzello (pp. 9, 17), Rex Features via AP Images (pp. 21, 29), Joel Ryan (pp. 5, 23), Richard Shotwell/Invision (p. 12), Sipa via AP Images (p. 19), Jordan Strauss/Invision (p. 27); *Getty Images*: Fred Duval/FilmMagic (p. 25), 20th Century-Fox (p. 11); *Shutterstock*: Richard Cavalleri (p. 7).

Library of Congress Cataloging-in-Publication Data

Tieck, Sarah, 1976-
 Robert Downey Jr. : star of Iron Man / Sarah Tieck.
   pages cm. -- (Big buddy biographies)
 ISBN 978-1-62403-197-7
 1. Downey, Robert, 1965- Juvenile literature. 2. Actors--United States--Biography--Juvenile literature. I. Title.
 PN2287.D548T63 2013
 791.4302'8092--dc23
 [B]
                          2013031965

Robert
Downey Jr.

Contents

Screen Star

Robert Downey Jr. is a talented actor. He is famous for starring in the Iron Man and Avengers movies. Robert is also known for his skillful acting in many other films. He has won awards for his work.

Fans get very excited to see Robert at movie openings.

Where in the World?

CANADA

N W E S

New York

Vermont

Maine

New Hampshire

Massachusetts

Pennsylvania

Rhode Island

Connecticut

New York City

ATLANTIC OCEAN

New Jersey

Family Ties

Robert John Downey Jr. was born in New York City, New York, on April 4, 1965. His parents are Elsie and Robert Sr. His sister is Allyson.

Growing up, Robert learned about acting and movies from his parents. His mother was an actress. And, his father made movies. Usually, he worked behind the camera.

6

Robert lived in a part of New York City called Greenwich Village. Many actors and artists live and work there.

Growing Up

Robert began acting **professionally** at a young age. In 1970, his father gave him his first part in a movie called *Pound*. All the actors played dogs. Robert had small parts in many of his father's movies.

Around 1978, Robert's parents divorced. Robert moved to Los Angeles, California, with his father. A couple years later, he left school and returned to New York.

Robert's mother taught her son to love acting.

Working Actor

In the 1980s, Robert took a variety of **roles**. In 1984, he acted in the movie *Firstborn*. From 1985 to 1986, he was on *Saturday Night Live*. In 1987, he had his first leading part. He acted in *The Pick-up Artist* with Molly Ringwald.

But, it was another 1987 movie that helped people truly see Robert's acting skills. In *Less Than Zero*, Robert played a man with a drug **addiction**. He starred with Andrew McCarthy.

In *The Pick-up Artist*, Robert's character, Jack Jericho, falls in love with Molly Ringwald's character, Randy Jensen.

Young Talent

By the 1990s, Robert was popular with fans. His acting talent earned him more **roles**. In 1991, he acted in *Soapdish*. For this movie, Robert worked with famous actors Sally Field, Kevin Kline, and Whoopi Goldberg.

Sally (*left*), Kevin (*below*), and Whoopi (*right*) are known for their acting skills. Robert was honored to work with them.

In 1992, Robert starred in *Chaplin*. He played famous actor Charlie Chaplin through a variety of ages. People noticed Robert's strong acting. They saw that he could be both serious and funny. They said he had a wide acting range.

In 1993, Robert was nominated for an Academy Award. This honor led to more roles. Each one helped him improve his skills and range. Robert was considered one of the most talented young actors.

Robert (*right*) changed his appearance to look like Charlie Chaplin (*below*). He also learned to move like the famous actor.

Dark Times

Robert was finding success as an actor. Yet he struggled with drug **addiction**. He first tried drugs around age eight. His addiction grew worse over the years.

Robert continued acting, but drugs caused problems for him. He hurt people he loved, lost work, and went to jail. He worked hard to overcome his addiction. By 2005, he had changed. His life and his acting improved!

When Robert was overcoming his drug addiction, actor Mel Gibson helped him. They are still close friends. In 2011, Mel presented him with an acting award.

Superhero

In 2008, Robert starred as Tony Stark in *Iron Man*. This movie is about Tony becoming a superhero. It made a lot of money, and people were excited about Robert's work.

That same year, Robert appeared in a funny movie called *Tropic Thunder*. People said his acting was bold. Robert was up for many important acting awards.

Robert acted in *Iron Man 2* in 2010.

Iron Man

Tony Stark is a man who becomes the superhero Iron Man. Tony is very smart and builds a special suit of armor. When he's wearing it, he can fly and is very strong. Iron Man is part of a team of superheroes called the Avengers.

The stories about Iron Man come from Marvel Comics. Comic book writer Stan Lee created the character in the 1960s.

Actors may have to film a scene
many times to get it just right.

Stan Lee is famous for creating many Marvel
Comics characters, including Spider-Man and Thor.
He often appears in the movies based on them.

Blockbusters

Soon, Robert got another big movie **role**. In 2009, he starred in *Sherlock Holmes*. The movie was a hit! Robert was up for more awards. Robert returned to this part in 2011 for *Sherlock Holmes: A Game of Shadows*.

In 2012, Robert appeared as Tony Stark again. This time, he acted in *The Avengers*. People were very excited for this movie. They loved Robert's work as the character Tony Stark.

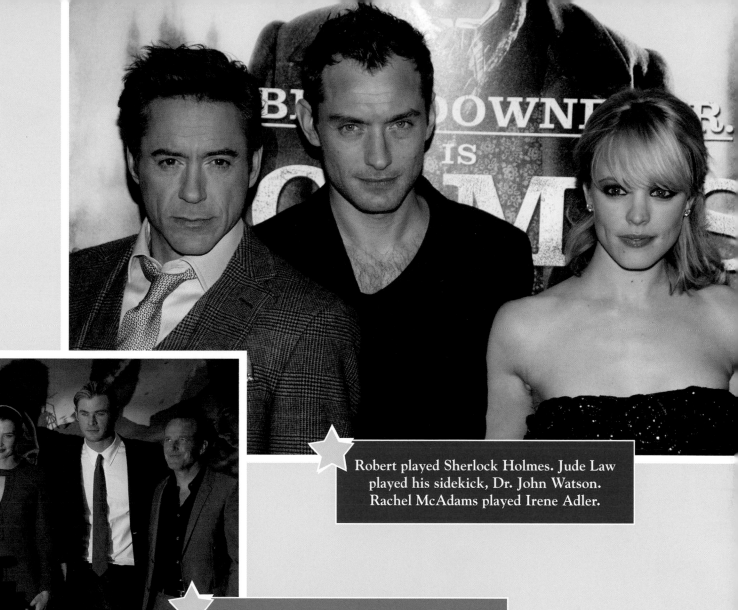

Robert played Sherlock Holmes. Jude Law played his sidekick, Dr. John Watson. Rachel McAdams played Irene Adler.

The Avengers is about a team of superheroes. They work together to save the earth.

An Actor's Life

As an actor, Robert spends time practicing **lines** and **performing**. He may be on a movie **set** for several hours each day. Sometimes he learns to do **stunts**.

Robert often travels to make or **promote** his movies. He also attends events and meets fans. He may be away from home for several days or even months.

Robert changes his appearance to look more like his characters. This includes wearing makeup and costumes!

Off the Screen

When Robert is not working, he spends time with his wife and sons. He enjoys being at home. Also, he studies Wing Chun kung fu.

Robert likes to help others. He has **volunteered** his time to help groups he supports. These include Global Zero and March of Dimes.

Robert's wife is Susan Downey. Their son Exton was born in 2012. Robert also has a grown-up son named Indio.

Buzz

In 2013, Robert returned to the role of Tony Stark in *Iron Man 3*. He planned to appear in another Avengers film in 2015. It is called *The Avengers: Age of Ultron*.

Robert continues to grow as an actor. Fans look forward to the roles he'll try next!

In *Iron Man 3*, Tony Stark's suit is even more powerful.

Snapshot

★**Name**: Robert John Downey Jr.

★**Birthday**: April 4, 1965

★**Birthplace**: New York City, New York

★**Appearances**: *Pound, Firstborn, Saturday Night Live, The Pick-up Artist, Less Than Zero, Soapdish, Chaplin, Iron Man, Tropic Thunder, Sherlock Holmes, Iron Man 2, Sherlock Holmes: A Game of Shadows, The Avengers, Iron Man 3, The Avengers: Age of Ultron*

Important Words

Academy Award an award given by the Academy of Motion Picture Arts and Sciences to the best actors and filmmakers of the year.

addiction a strong need or want for a substance, activity, or other thing.

lines the words an actor says in a play, a movie, or a show.

nominate to name as a possible winner.

perform to do something in front of an audience.

professional (pruh-FEHSH-nuhl) working for money rather than only for pleasure.

promote to help something become known.

role a part an actor plays.

set the place where a movie or a television show is recorded.

stunt an action requiring great skill or daring.

volunteer (vah-luhn-TIHR) to help others in one's free time without pay.

Web Sites

To learn more about Robert Downey Jr., visit ABDO Publishing Company online. Web sites about Robert Downey Jr. are featured on our Book Links page. These links are routinely monitored and updated to provide the most current information available.

www.abdopublishing.com

Index